JOE NAMATH

by
William R. Sanford
&
Carl R. Green

CRESTWOOD HOUSE
New York

Maxwell Macmillan Canada
Toronto

Maxwell Macmillan International
New York Oxford Singapore Sydney

Library of Congress Cataloging-in-Publication Data
Sanford, William R. (William Reynolds), 1927–
   Joe Namath / by William R. Sanford and Carl R. Green. — 1st ed.
     p. cm. — (Sports immortals)
   Includes bibliographical references and index.
   ISBN 0-89686-782-X
     1. Namath, Joe Willie, 1943– —Juvenile literature. 2. Football players—United States—Biography—Juvenile literature.
I. Green, Carl R. II. Title. III. Series.
GV939.N28S26   1993
796.332'092—dc20
   [B]   92-26324

Photo Credits
All photos courtesy of AP—Wide World Photos.

CRESTWOOD HOUSE

Macmillan Publishing Company
866 Third Avenue
New York, NY 10022

Maxwell Macmillan Canada, Inc.
1200 Eglinton Avenue East
Suite 200
Don Mills, Ontario M3C 3N1

Macmillan Publishing Company is part of the Maxwell Communication Group of Companies.

Produced by Flying Fish Studio

Printed in the United States of America

First edition

10 9 8 7 6 5 4 3 2 1

CONTENTS

AN END AND A BEGINNING

The University of Alabama was picked to play Texas in Miami's Orange Bowl on New Year's Day, 1965. Led by **quarterback** Joe Namath, the undefeated Crimson Tide of Alabama reigned as the nation's top college football team. But Alabama's coach Paul "Bear" Bryant started Steve Sloan as quarterback. The reason was easy to see. Joe had been limping badly during pregame warmups.

Texas jumped ahead with two quick touchdowns in the first quarter. Coach Bryant saw the game slipping away. Early in the second quarter he sent Joe in to replace Sloan. Six complete passes closed the gap to 14–7. But Texas roared back to score a third **touchdown (TD)**. At halftime the scoreboard read Texas 21, Alabama 7.

The Tide struck for ten more points in the third quarter. Joe threw a second TD pass and the Alabama kicker hit a field goal. Faced with the surging Alabama offense, the Longhorns tried to dig in. Less than two minutes remained when Alabama rolled to a first-and-goal on the six-yard line.

As the clock clicked off the final seconds, the huge crowd held its breath. Could the Tide's miracle-working quarterback finish off the comeback he had inspired? With the game on the line, Joe called three running plays. The Texas defenders bent but did not break. On fourth down, Joe carried the ball himself. He found a tiny hole and wedged himself into the end zone. An official raised his arms to signal a touchdown. But a second official grabbed the ball and placed it on the six-inch line. The game ended seconds later. Texas won by those six inches, 21–17.

As he left the field, Joe told his coach that he knew he had scored. "If you can't jam it in from there without leaving any doubt, you don't deserve to win," the Bear snapped.

The pain of the loss did not last. Joe learned that he had been voted the game's Most Valuable Player. Then he appeared at a news conference with Sonny Werblin, owner of the New York Jets. Werblin was convinced that Joe could win games and sell tickets for his pro football team. He backed up his faith with a three-year contract worth $420,000. That made Joe the highest paid rookie ever signed to play pro football.

To complete the deal, the Jets owner gave Joe a $7,000 Lincoln Continental. The Lincoln took the place of Joe's half share in a rattletrap 1952 Ford. From that day on, the poor kid from Beaver Falls, Pennsylvania, rode in style.

TRIVIA 1*

Beaver Falls gave Joe his high school football jersey when it celebrated Joe Namath Day in 1969. Why was Joe so pleased by the award?

* Answers to all Trivia Quiz questions can be found on pages 46–47.

Alabama quarterback Joe Namath (right) *signs a contract to play pro football with the New York Jets. Coach Weeb Ewbank* (left) *and team owner Sonny Werblin* (center) *have high hopes for their star rookie.*

GROWING UP IN PENNSYLVANIA

John and Rose Namath's fourth child was born on May 31, 1943. Rose's doctor had promised that after three sons (Sonny, Bobby and Franklin) she was certain to have a girl. That was good news to Rose, who had already painted the baby's room pink. She forgot about baby girls, however, when she saw her new son's blue-green eyes, dimples and long black hair. The Namaths named him Joseph William Namath in honor of their Hungarian parents.

The Namaths lived in a two-story house on Sixth Street in Beaver Falls, Pennsylvania. Money was scarce in the small steel-mill town. John worked long hours in the heat of the mills. Joe wore his brothers' hand-me-downs. When the boy was six, his parents adopted 12-year-old Rita. Rose had a daughter to cherish, and the family was complete.

Skinny little Joe thought Beaver Falls was a great place to grow up. Close at hand lay a river, a woods, a junkyard, some factories and a laundry. His best friend, Linny Alford, lived across the street. The two boys played, ate and worked together. Rose hardly noticed that Linny was black. However, she did put her foot down the day Joe decided he wanted to be black too. Scrubbing off the brown shoe polish he had smeared on his face was a tough job.

Joe learned his ABCs at St. Mary's Grammar School. During the school year the nuns kept Joe and Linny busy. It was the summers that worried Rose and John. With time on their hands, the boys were seldom far from trouble. Rose's heart almost stopped the day she saw Joe and Linny dangling beneath a railroad bridge. The boys held on while a train rumbled past and then climbed to safety. The prank earned Joe a good spanking.

When they were seven, Joe and Linny started their own business. First they failed as shoeshine boys. Their customers complained that the boys left more polish on their pants than on their shoes. A plan to sell fishing worms ended when Rose found a box of night crawlers in her icebox. But the boys did not quit. Soon they were selling household discards to the local junkman. That venture ended when the parents learned that Joe and Linny were selling the same junk over and over. The trick lay in reclaiming yesterday's junk before the junkyard opened each morning.

Joe discovered sports when he was ten. Basketball, football and baseball were soon taking up most of his time. Joe and Linny organized a **sandlot football** team with nine other black kids. The boys played every day after school and squeezed in more games on weekends. Rose guesses that the team won about 112 games against zero losses.

At home, the Namaths' family life was no longer the best. Joe's older brothers and his sister had grown up and moved out. John and Rose divorced in 1955. After that, Rose and Joe moved from one home to another. Through the bad times, Joe never complained. "Don't worry, Mom," he told Rose. "Things will be okay."

TRIVIA
2

Bear Bryant, Joe's coach at Alabama, coached many fine passers during his long career. What player did Coach Bryant rank as the greatest of all his quarterbacks?

HIGH SCHOOL HERO

Joe's goal as he grew up was to escape the steel mills. But the towns of western Pennsylvania offered few jobs outside of the mills. Joe's brother Sonny took one road out. Sonny joined the army as soon as he finished high school. Joe chose a different route. He planned to turn his athletic talents into a college scholarship. As each sport came in season, he practiced with his brothers. In the fall they taught him to throw a football. When spring came, they pitched batting practice and helped him sharpen his fielding.

At 14, Joe tried out for the junior high school football team. Before long the starting quarterback went down with a broken arm. Joe, a slender five-footer, took over as the number-one signal-caller. Opposing teams razzed him when he crouched low behind center, but the laughter soon stopped. In the first quarter of his first game Joe threw two touchdown passes. That summer a welcome growth spurt added 20 pounds and two much-needed inches.

Joe starred in three sports after he entered high school in 1958. As a tenth grader he made the varsity football team but rarely played. During Joe's junior year a new coach took over. Larry Bruno thought Joe had talent, but he gave the quarterback

 TRIVIA 3 Joe's critics often complain that he threw too many interceptions. How does his interception record of 5.85 percent (based on percentage of passes intercepted out of passes thrown) compare with the 49ers' Joe Montana?

10

Joe's relationship with his mother, Rose, was always a close and loving one.

job to a senior. Joe's playing time came mostly on defense. At last, in the final game of the season, Coach Bruno put Joe in on offense. Joe turned a close game into a rout with two quick TD passes.

By his senior year Joe had shot up to six feet and weighed 175 pounds. On the basketball court he joined four black players in the starting lineup. Agile and quick, he could dunk a basketball over much taller players. On the baseball field he hit a sparkling .450 and fielded like a pro.

But football was king in Pennsylvania. Joe worked hard to develop his game. His brother Bobby taught him proper footwork. From Coach Bruno Joe learned to fool the defense with clever ball handling. Thanks to his own quickness, he became adept at getting rid of the ball. His quick release often caught defenders out of position. Off the field, Coach Bruno badgered Joe to improve his grades. Joe won a milkshake from the coach by proving he could earn a B in math.

In the first game of 1960, Joe faked a handoff and hid the ball on his hip. The tricky move freed him to run 60 yards to a touchdown. The Tigers were unbeaten when they met their old rivals, New Castle High School. Beaver Falls had not scored against the powerful Hurricanes for nine years. With Joe leading the way, the Tigers rang up a shutout of their own, 39–0. The senior quarterback scored two TDs and completed nine of 13 passes.

The Tigers' 9–0 record brought the western Pennsylvania championship home to Beaver Falls. *Scholastic Coach* magazine picked Joe for its high school **All-American** team. Here was a young quarterback who completed 70 percent of his passes! Joe's mailbox was soon overflowing with college scholarship offers.

A PENNSYLVANIA BOY GOES SOUTH

Most high school athletes are happy if they receive two or three **scholarship** offers. Blue-chip quarterbacks are worth their weight in gold, however. Over 50 of the nation's colleges invited Joe to visit. Rose, who had remarried, thought back to her son's days as a Catholic altar boy. She steered him toward Notre Dame. Joe visited the Notre Dame campus but chose not to go to an all-boys school. He was looking forward to an active social life in college.

After touring a number of campuses, Joe picked the University of Maryland. Maryland's football coaches wanted him, but there was a catch. The school's freshmen had to score 750 on the **Scholastic Aptitude Test (SAT)**. Joe's failure to hit the books caught up with him. He may have been a football genius, but he scored only 730 on his first SAT. That summer, Joe studied harder than he ever had before. He improved his score—but fell three points short of the magic number. Maryland was out.

A few days later a **recruiter** from the University of Alabama dropped by. Howard Schnellenberger described the school, its football program and its famous coach, Paul "Bear" Bryant. Alabama, he said, wasn't worried about Joe's SAT score. Rose liked the idea of sending her carefree son to play for the no-nonsense Bryant.

Joe and Coach Schnellenberger drove south that same day. When they reached Tuscaloosa, Joe's new teammates did not know what to make of this flashy northerner. But Coach Bryant knew football talent when he saw it. The Bear put his rookie to work with the freshman team. By the end of the week Joe was running the complex offense like an old pro.

Coach Bryant shares a sad moment with Joe after a losing game.

The freshman team played only three games in 1961. Against Mississippi State, the Crimson Tide was sitting on a six-point lead. Late in the game, Joe found himself deep in his own end of the field. The scoreboard showed fourth down and three yards to go. Instead of **punting**, Joe called a little look-in pass. The play almost gave Joe's coach a heart attack, but the pass picked up a first down. The minutes gained by the surprise call saved the game. Time ran out with Mississippi on Alabama's four-yard line. In the big game against archrival Auburn, rain held the score down. Despite the slick ball, Joe threw the 46-yard touchdown pass that earned a 7–7 tie.

Success on the football field did not solve Joe's problems on Alabama's all-white campus. In those days, the college attracted few northerners. To southern students, Joe might have been from another planet. He talked and dressed strangely, they thought. Many of his classmates resented his easy acceptance of blacks. Joe brooded over the racial insults he heard. At one point he called home to say he was going to quit school.

His brother Franklin picked up the phone. "I'll tell you this just once," Franklin said. "Name-calling doesn't hurt anywhere near as much as the whipping you'll get if you come back here a quitter."

Joe agreed to stick it out. Perhaps his social life wasn't going well, but Coach Bryant's football program was on a roll. The Alabama varsity went undefeated that year. The team wrapped up the national championship with a Sugar Bowl victory over Arkansas.

TRIVIA 4 — In 1967 Joe set a pro football record by passing for 4,007 yards. How does that total compare with the current record?

WINNING A NATIONAL CHAMPIONSHIP

Pro baseball teams knocked on Joe's door during his freshman year. When the Chicago Cubs increased their offer to $50,000, Joe was ready to sign. At that point Coach Bryant brought in Bubba Church. The former pitcher convinced Joe that big leaguers have short careers. Where would he be then without a college degree? The money would be gone and he'd be stoking a steel-mill furnace.

In time, Joe began to make friends at Alabama. He learned to enjoy the slower pace and natural beauty of the deep South. Soon Joe was dressing like his classmates and talking with a southern accent. Because many of his new friends had two first names, he took to calling himself Joe Willie.

Joe played his first varsity game against Georgia on September 22, 1962. He calmly connected for a 52-yard touchdown pass on his fourth play. Before the day was over, Joe had added two more TD passes. That tied an Alabama record.

Seven games later, Alabama took its unbeaten record into a game with Georgia Tech. The hitting was fierce and neither side could get its offense going. With Georgia Tech leading 7–6, Joe engineered a last-minute drive that carried to Tech's 14-yard line. A short field goal would very likely win the game. At that key moment Coach Bryant took Joe out of the game. Dreams of another national championship vanished when the new quarterback threw an **interception**. Some of the pain was eased on New Year's Day during the Orange Bowl. Joe sparkled in a 17–0 win over a strong Oklahoma team.

The 1963 season turned into something of a downer for Joe. Florida beat the Tide 10–6, and Auburn upset them 10–8. For Joe, there was worse to come. He began to party too hard after Saturday's games. When Coach Bryant learned Joe had been drinking, he suspended him from the team. With Steve Sloan running the offense, Alabama beat Miami and upset Ole Miss in the Sugar Bowl.

Joe regained his first-string position during spring practice. That fall he turned into a running and passing demon. In the first two games he ran for five TDs and led the nation in scoring. Disaster struck in the fourth game. On the first play of the second quarter he rolled out to his right, ready to run or pass. As he cut back, his right knee collapsed. Later, Joe said of the pain, "I thought I'd been shot."

The knee mended, but Joe was in and out of the lineup for the rest of the season. Against Georgia Tech he came in 90 seconds before the half. Joe's passes moved the ball to the one-yard line, and a runner carried it in from there. Coach Bryant then called for an on-sides kick and Alabama recovered. Joe limped back to the huddle and drove the Tide to a second TD. The game ended 21–7, and Alabama had won another national championship. Even though the Tide lost the 1965 Orange Bowl game, the national title was theirs to keep.

With the season over, Joe looked forward to a bright future. The $420,000 contract he signed with the Jets took care of money worries. Now the challenge of pro football lay ahead. How would Jets coach Weeb Ewbank compare to his high school and college coaches? Coach Bryant would be hard to match, he thought. "I just believe [Bryant's] not only a great coach, but a great man," Joe said.

AFL ROOKIE OF THE YEAR

Sonny Werblin's New York Jets belonged to the American Football League (AFL). In 1965 the league was locked in a make-or-break struggle with the older National Football League (NFL). Werblin believed that the AFL needed the best players around if it was to survive. After signing his new quarterback, he waved the big numbers in Joe's contract like a flag. Reporters, who made less than a tenth as much per year, tended to be skeptical. Was any rookie worth that much money?

On the plane taking Joe to New York, a sportswriter asked, "What did you study at Alabama, Joe? Basket weaving?"

Joe's smile was dazzling. "No," he shot back. "Basket weaving was too hard. They put me in **journalism**."

In New York, the Jets team doctor operated on Joe's knee. After the surgery Joe worked out with weights to rebuild strength in the knee. As he said later, the knee was a pain, but it kept him out of the army. In 1965 the Vietnam War was raging and young men Joe's age were being drafted. After he failed his third physical, the draft board listed him 4-F, unfit for duty.

The Jets opened their training camp at Peekskill, New York, in July. Some of his teammates gave him a bad time. Joe told them to judge him by how he played, not by what he was paid. If he lived up to his contract, he assured them, they would all make plenty of money. Back in New York City, the fans were voting with their wallets. Thanks to Joe, the Jets doubled their season ticket sales.

Coach Ewbank planned to bring his prize rookie along slowly. Joe sat out the first game, a loss to Houston. For the home opener, Werblin ordered Ewbank to give Joe some playing time. The Shea Stadium fans booed when quarterback Mike Taliaferro misfired on some passes. The boos changed to cheers when Joe entered the game. Almost at once Joe threw a TD pass to Don Maynard. The Jets lost that night, but the fans didn't seem to care. The team's new quarterback was a threat to score from anywhere on the field.

For a time Joe threw as many interceptions as he did touchdowns. Pro defenses were hard to read and pro defenders were fast and skillful. Then came the breakthrough. In a rematch against Houston, Joe completed 17 of 26 passes. Four of the passes went for touchdowns.

In that up-and-down year the Jets won only five games. Five victories didn't win any titles, but the team had won the hearts of its fans. Joe ended the year with 164 completions, good for 2,200 yards and 18 touchdowns. Those stats earned him AFL Rookie of the Year honors.

Joe worked hard to merit his high salary and prove himself to fans and teammates.

Joe sits dejectedly on the bench after being intercepted for a touchdown.

Joe injured his knee again during the 1966 preseason. Despite the pain, he played in every game that year and led the AFL in passing. His 232 completions were good for 3,379 yards and 19 TDs. In 1967 Joe proved that his fine sophomore year was not a fluke. His 258 completions led the AFL and his 4,007 passing yards led all of pro football. Sadly, the Jets' record improved more slowly. The team went 6–6–2 in 1966 and 8–5–1 in 1967. Then, in 1968, Joe and his teammates put a year together that made football history.

A SUPER BOWL GUARANTEE

The New York Jets came of age in 1968. The team won the AFL's Eastern Division with an 11–3 record. Joe completed 187 passes for 2,734 yards and 19 TDs. Only the Oakland Raiders stood between the Jets and Super Bowl III.

Shea Stadium was packed when the teams met two days after Christmas. With a cold wind swirling around the field, Joe went

During the first quarter of this AFL championship game, Joe sends the ball off in a high-flying pass.

to work. By halftime the Jets had built a slim 13–10 lead, but the price was high. Joe was groggy from a near concussion. He had dislocated a finger and his knees were sore. His sub warmed up but Joe refused to leave the game.

Oakland moved ahead in the fourth quarter, 23–20. On the next series Joe looked deep for Don Maynard, his favorite receiver. The **bomb** was good for a 52-yard gain. Then, from the six-yard line, Maynard made a sliding catch of Joe's low pass. The TD was enough to send the Jets to the **Super Bowl**.

In 1968 the Super Bowl was only two years old. Twice the NFL's Green Bay Packers had smashed the AFL's teams. Until an AFL team won the big game it would always be the "funny little league." The betting line on Super Bowl III made it clear that no one expected an upset. Las Vegas installed the NFL's Baltimore Colts as 17-point favorites.

Joe was not impressed by what he saw in the Colts' game films. He spoke out loudly and often. First he said that at least four AFL quarterbacks were better than the Colts' Earl Morrall. Then he went out on a very thin limb. "We're going to win the Super Bowl," he announced. "I *guarantee* it." The Colts shrugged and prepared for their victory party. Lou Michaels, the Colt kicker, sent Joe a dozen roses.

When the whistle blew on January 12, 1969, the Jets' game plan shocked the Colts. Prepared for a passing attack, they did not expect Joe to call running back Matt Snell's number. Snell took Joe's handoffs and rumbled through and around the Colt defense. When the defenders moved up to stop the run, Joe threw deep to Maynard. Meanwhile, the Colt offense was misfiring. The Jets ran into the locker room at halftime with a 7–0 lead.

Quarterbacks Joe Namath (left) *of the New York Jets and Earl Morrall* (right) *of the Baltimore Colts*

Joe keeps a watchful eye on his opponents as he passes the ball to running back Bill Mathis during this 1969 Super Bowl game.

The Colts moved the ball in the second half, but their own mistakes kept them from scoring. In the meantime Joe moved the Jets into position for two Jim Turner **field goals**. New York now led 13–0. At that point the Colts replaced Morrall with Johnny Unitas. Johnny U cranked up his sore arm as best he could. He finally led the Colts to a score, but only after Turner had kicked a third field goal. Three minutes later the Jets were Super Bowl champs, 16–7. No one was laughing at the AFL now.

Joe was everyone's pick as the game's Most Valuable Player. As Billy Ray Smith of the Colts said, "Joe did it all. He had it all going, and so they won." The victory also earned Joe the Hickok Belt as the top pro athlete of 1969.

Later, after a wild team party, the Jets returned to New York. No one thought to pick up the Super Bowl trophy from the hotel safe. Joe didn't care. He was on top of the world.

THE LEGEND OF BROADWAY JOE

New York loved Joe from the day he stepped off the airplane. Sonny Werblin had advised his new star on how to handle himself. Joe didn't need much coaching. His style on and off the field appealed to New Yorkers.

Reporters flocked to interview the handsome young star. After one game, Joe stayed in the showers to avoid the post-game questions. That didn't stop one eager sportswriter. The man stepped into the shower and interviewed Joe there. The newspapers ran stories about Joe's social life, his bachelor apartment and his sex appeal. About that time *Sports Illustrated* ran a cover showing Joe framed by the lights of Times Square. From that day on he was "Broadway Joe."

Broadway Joe gets fitted for a new mink coat valued at $5,000.

With fame came new ways to make money. Joe was given a $5,000 mink as his fee for modeling the coat. When thieves stole the mink, he refused to be upset. "Never had it on again," he said. In 1968 he grew a drooping mustache. League officials were not thrilled. They told him that long hair and mustaches gave the AFL a bad image. For a time Joe refused to shave the mustache. Then an electric-razor company offered him $10,000 to shave the mustache on national television. Joe went in front of the cameras, shaved and collected his check.

With money rolling in, Joe looked for investments. Along with two friends, he bought a nightclub and named it Bachelors III. In the spring of 1969 football commissioner Pete Rozelle ordered Joe to sell the club. Bachelors III, Rozelle said, had become a hangout for gamblers. Joe called a news conference and said he would quit football rather than sell.

Sportscasters gather to attend the press conference in which Joe announced his retirement from football.

A relieved football commissioner Pete Rozelle joins Joe at a news conference in which Namath announces his decision to sell the restaurant and return to the Jets.

At first, both sides refused to back down. Then, as the football season neared, Joe decided to sell. Giving up football was too high a price to pay. Later, he said, "I learned a pretty good lesson over a lousy nightclub. The lesson was that life isn't going to be fair all the time. And you know, so what? You can't make it fair, so you move on."

TRIVIA 5

If Joe hadn't signed to play for the Jets in 1965, what NFL team was equally eager to sign him?

The popular Jets star was often interviewed on radio and television.

Women admired Joe's green eyes, warm smile and graceful slouch. Some of the women he met handed Joe their phone numbers. To his coach's dismay, Joe also liked Johnnie Walker Red whiskey. Women and whiskey, he claimed, took away tension.

Joe began each day by waking up around 11 o'clock. Afternoons were for practice and watching game films. In the early evening he napped, watched a movie or wrote letters. Then, when most people were ready for sleep, Joe went out on the town. At about 3:00 A.M., after hitting a nightclub or two, he headed home to bed. "I'm just a normal guy who keeps an abnormal schedule," Joe explained.

Beaver Falls proclaimed May 24, 1969, Joe Namath Day. After honoring Joe with a parade, the mayor gave him the keys to the city. The high school retired his Number 19 jersey. Joe showed his thanks by announcing the first Joe Namath Scholarship. Then he headed for the airport. Back in New York there was money to be made and football games to be played.

A CAREER WINDS DOWN

Joe quarterbacked the Jets for seven years after his Super Bowl triumph. Despite his passing and play-calling, the team never made it back to the top. Only once did the Jets win more games than they lost. Critics said they were a jewel box designed to show off one sparkling star. The "star" had his problems too. Joe had always thrown too many interceptions. With a weaker team behind him, he could not always overcome those crippling **turnovers**.

Joe prepares to make a pass at the ten-yard line during a game against the Houston Oilers.

Despite his problems, sportswriters rated Joe as one of the game's great quarterbacks. What records would he have set if he had played on healthy knees? No one would ever know. Joe played only five games in 1970 because of injuries. In 1971 he went down again after a tackle by Detroit's Mike Lucci. He played only four games that season. Even so, in a game against San Francisco he showed flashes of his old form. In less than two quarters Joe rifled three TD passes through the strong 49er defense.

Joe completes a pass for a six-yard gain against the San Francisco 49ers.

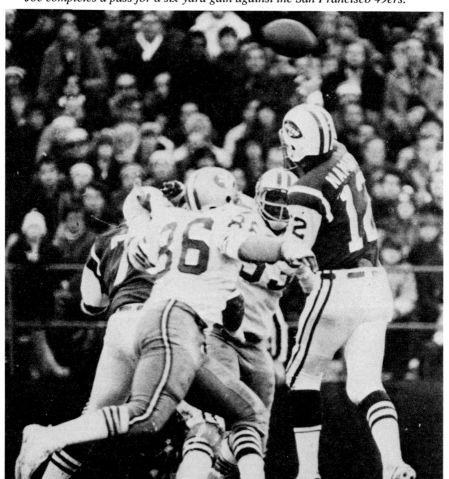

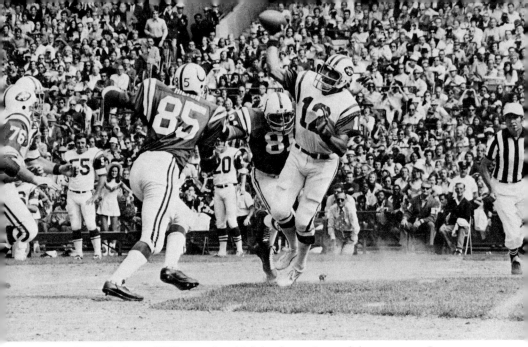

Here, during a 1972 game in which he threw six touchdown passes, Joe leads the Jets to a 44–34 victory against the Baltimore Colts.

Joe bounced back in 1972. Inspired by a two-year, $500,000 contract, he led the AFL in passing yardage and TD passes. The team's improved play did not carry over to 1973. Joe went down with a shoulder injury in the second game. Don Maynard was gone and Coach Ewbank was on his way out. Joe took a pounding in every game. One Sunday, after a blitzing linebacker knocked him down, he scolded his linemen. "I picked up the linebacker that time," he snapped. "How about you guys getting the next one?"

Before each game, trainers drained fluid from Joe's knees. The sight of the long needle made some of his teammates feel faint. Even so, Number 12 could still make the great plays. In November 1974 the Jets were trailing the Giants by a touchdown. Joe called a **bootleg** around left end. His fake sent the Giants veering right and Joe limped safely into the end zone. A Giants coach said, "He looked like a guy with two wooden legs. It was like slow motion. It took a lot of courage to play with that."

Mean and lean quarterback machine Joe Namath calls the winning plays.

Joe's career was nearing its end. In November 1976 Coach Lou Holtz benched him in favor of Richard Todd. Joe had to agree that Todd was younger and more mobile. Released during the off-season, Joe signed with the Los Angeles Rams. Playing for the Rams, he hoped, would give him one last shot at the Super Bowl. It was an older and wiser Joe Namath who reported to training camp in 1977. The Ram trainers sent him to a swimming pool to exercise. Working out in the pool helped him get in shape without straining his knees.

Joe's roommate, quarterback Pat Haden, reported that Joe no longer cruised the night spots. On most nights, Haden said, "we made a bowl of popcorn and watched the 11 o'clock news. Then we watched Johnny Carson and went to sleep after the monologue."

The Ram coaches liked Joe's quick arm and his ability to read defenses. But the team started badly. Joe was benched after he completed only 16 of 40 passes against the Chicago Bears. Playing as young Haden's backup, Joe rode the bench for the last two months. When the season ended he knew it was time to go. Joe announced his retirement early in 1978.

TRIVIA 6

Joe woke up one day to find his name on a list compiled by President Richard Nixon's White House. On what list did Nixon's office staff put Joe's name?

Joe may have been retired but he was still in demand. In 1975 he signed a multimillion dollar contract to appear in all advertising connected with a new line of sportswear, the Joe Namath Signature Collection.

AN ACTIVE RETIREMENT

Joe was only 35 years old when he retired from football. Except for his knees, he was still a young man. With most of his life ahead of him he looked for new worlds to conquer.

Acting gave Joe one outlet for his talents. As far back as 1968 he had appeared in a film called *Norwood*. A year later he was cast opposite Ann-Margret in *C.C. Rider and Company*. Joe played a motorcycle rider in that one. He also appeared in *The Last Rebel* and *Chattanooga Choo Choo*. None of the films won much applause from the critics. His 1978 television sitcom, "The Waverly Wonders," was canceled after only four weeks. On stage, Joe has earned greater acceptance. His favorite play is the musical comedy *Guys and Dolls*.

"I love the theater," Joe says. "It's the only thing I've found that compares with the rush of **adrenaline** when you were in the tunnel waiting to play a game. You're alive, the audience is alive, you're putting yourself on the line."

Chatting with other cast members on location while filming Norwood

At a press conference with Roone Arledge (center), *president of ABC News and Sports, and former football great Frank Gifford* (right) *after Joe signed on with ABC's "Monday Night Football"*

Everywhere Joe went, he drew a crowd of adoring fans. Television tried to cash in on that feeling. In 1985 ABC hired him for "Monday Night Football." The job ended with Joe being released after a year. In a second trial on NBC Sports he proved that he had the stuff to be a good broadcaster. For that job, he trained as hard as he had for a football season. Now fans can see him each fall, walking the sidelines and talking to coaches and players. If someone makes a mistake, Joe is likely to point it out.

34

Following his short career with ABC, Joe joined the NBC sports broadcasting staff in 1986. He can still be found reporting on the season's games.

Many quarterbacks, including Richard Todd (right), *looked toward Joe Namath as a role model on the playing field.*

Long before Joe retired he ran a football camp each summer. He still takes an active role, both as teacher and counselor. Most years, he is on hand from the first day to the last. Joe enjoys the contact with the young players. When he works with the quarterbacks, everyone stops to watch. The old magic is still there.

In 1969 Joe teamed with Dick Schaap to write a book about his life. The young Broadway Joe called the book, *I Can't Wait Until Tomorrow... 'Cause I Get Better-Looking Every Day.* If Joe were to write a book today, the title would be more modest. His life is slower and calmer. He lives on a five-acre farm in Connecticut, complete with horses, cats and dogs. Money is no problem, for he has invested wisely. He spends much of his time with his wife, Deborah, and his daughter, Jessica.

Football was good to Joe, but he paid a high price for his fame. In 1992, at age 48, he was limping like a 90-year-old man. Surgery was the only answer. Doctors replaced both knees in a four-hour operation. With luck and hard work, Joe figures, he'll soon be walking without pain.

As Joe says, "You've seen a four-month-old puppy running around looking to get into anything. Then he gets older and he doesn't look so hard. That's the way I am now."

TRIVIA 7

Each year sportswriters award the Heisman Trophy to the nation's outstanding college football player. In 1964 Joe led Alabama to a national championship and an undefeated season. Despite Joe's brilliant year, the Heisman was given to another quarterback. Who was the winner?

Joe poses with a bronze bust of himself after his induction into the Pro Football Hall of Fame in Canton, Ohio.

JOE NAMATH, FOOTBALL IMMORTAL

The Pro Football Hall of Fame is reserved for the greatest players the game has produced. Joe Namath became a member in 1985. Even so, some experts rank him behind such quarterbacks as Bart Starr and Roger Staubach. When it comes to won-and-lost records, that may be a fair judgment. But Joe did something no other quarterback has done. His "guaranteed" victory in Super Bowl III saved the AFL. After that upset win the NFL had to accept the younger league as an equal.

TRIVIA 8 On November 17, 1968, Joe threw for 381 yards, but the Jets lost a squeaker to the Oakland Raiders. Why do football fans still speak of that as "the Heidi Game"?

Modern football players owe a second debt to Joe. The success of the AFL led to a merge with the NFL in 1970, which turned pro football into a money machine. Television networks lined up to pay huge sums for the right to televise the games. With the money rolling in, the players could ask for bigger salaries. Today's top **draft** picks demand—and receive—million-dollar contracts. Veteran stars earn even more.

One way to judge Joe is to remember his style. Joe wore long hair and white shoes when no one else did. He was "cool." If a company wanted to pay him big bucks to model panty hose, he did it. He was Broadway Joe and everyone knew he was no sissy. Like Babe Ruth, he was bigger than life. Even his critics had to admire his courage and his talent.

Joe earned big bucks as the spokesman for Eclipse Laboratories at-home shaving products.

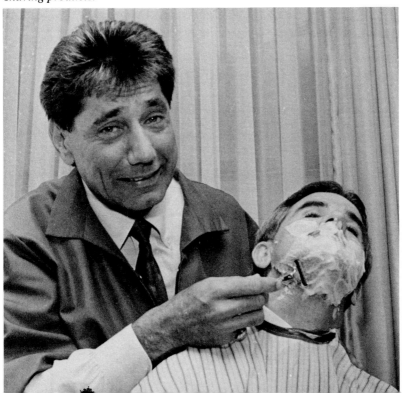

Weeb Ewbank (right) *and Joe share a moment at the announcement of Ewbank's retirement after 25 years of service to football.*

Vince Lombardi, the great Green Bay coach, was a Namath fan. "Joe Namath," Lombardi said, "is the greatest pure thrower of footballs I have ever seen." The hard-nosed Lombardi knew that Joe left his playboy habits behind when he suited up. Joe was a student of the game. He studied game films and compiled thick notebooks on defensive players. Many of the Jets' plays were based on Joe's suggestions. Best of all, he inspired his teammates. "When Joe comes into the huddle, you believe he can do it for you," said guard Randy Rasmussen. "You might believe other people, but you believe him more."

Another tribute came from opposing teams. After the first few years, defensive players seldom tackled him below the waist. Even when he was killing them with his passes, no one wanted to injure his fragile knees. Joe Gilliam, a rival quarterback, spoke for players and fans alike when he said, "[Joe's] got guts. He's got more guts than any player in the game."

TRIVIA 9

How many all-time pro football passing records does Joe Namath hold?

Joe Namath will long be remembered for his good looks, flashy personality and skillful moves on the football field.

TRIVIA 10 Each player on the Jets earned $15,000 for winning Super Bowl III. What was the winner's share in 1991's Super Bowl XXV?

GLOSSARY

adrenaline—A chemical produced by the adrenal gland that prepares the body for vigorous action.

All-American—An honorary team made up of the nation's best players at each position.

bomb—A football term for a long pass that gains 40 or more yards.

bootleg—A play in which the quarterback fakes the ball to a running back and then hides it. If the defense "bites" on the fake, the quarterback is free to pass or run the ball for a big gain.

draft—A process by which pro teams take turns selecting the top college players. If a player wants to play in the NFL, he must sign with the team that drafted him.

field goal—A scoring play in which one player holds the ball on the ground while a second player kicks it between the goal posts. A successful field goal adds three points to the kicking team's score.

interception—A play in which a defensive player catches a pass intended for an offensive player.

journalism—A course of study that teaches students how to write news stories.

punt—A play in which the offensive team kicks the ball as far down the field as it can. A well-executed punt leaves the opposing team deep in its own territory.

quarterback—The key player in the offensive backfield. A quarterback calls the plays, handles the ball and does most of the passing.

43

recruiters—Members of a college staff who try to sign up top high school athletes to play football for their school.

sandlot football—Pickup games organized by neighborhood kids. The games are usually played without adult supervision.

scholarship—Financial aid given to an athlete who agrees to play football for a college or university.

Scholastic Aptitude Test (SAT)—A test taken by high school seniors to prove they have the ability to succeed in college.

Super Bowl—The yearly playoff game between the two conferences (the AFC and the NFC) of the National Football League. The first Super Bowl was played in 1967.

touchdown (TD)—A scoring play in which a player is judged to have possession of the ball in the opponent's end zone. Most TDs are scored when a player carries the ball across the goal line or catches a pass in the end zone. A touchdown adds six points to the offensive team's score.

turnover—Any play in which the offensive team gives up the ball to the defense on a fumble, interception or other mistake.

MORE GOOD READING ABOUT JOE NAMATH

Burchard, Marshall. *Sports Hero: Joe Namath.* New York: G. P. Putnam's Sons, 1971.

Green, Jerry. "The Guarantee," *Super Bowl Chronicles.* Grand Rapids, MI: Masters Press, 1991.

Namath, Joe. *Football for Young Players and Parents.* New York: Simon & Schuster, 1986.

Namath, Joe Willie, with Dick Schaap. *I Can't Wait Until Tomorrow… 'Cause I Get Better-Looking Every Day.* New York: Random House, 1969.

Ralbovsky, Martin. *The Namath Effect.* Englewood Cliffs, NJ: Prentice-Hall, 1976.

Szolnoki, Rose Namath, with Bill Kushner. *Namath: My Son Joe.* Birmingham, AL: Oxmoor House, 1975.

Telander, Rick. *Joe Namath and the Other Guys.* New York: Holt, Rinehart and Winston, 1976.

JOE NAMATH TRIVIA QUIZ

1: Joe had always wanted to keep his Number 19 jersey. In 1960, Coach Bruno had promised Joe and his teammates that they could keep their jerseys. He broke his promise when it became clear that the school couldn't afford to buy new ones.

2: Coach Bryant greatly admired Joe's passing skills, but he ranked Ken Stabler ahead of him. Stabler went on to star for the Oakland Raiders during the 1970s.

3: Joe Montana is rated as one of the all-time best at avoiding interceptions. The defense picks off only 2.68 percent of his passes. Broadway Joe's defenders are quick to point out that the Jets' style of play called for him to throw longer (and riskier) passes.

4: Dan Marino of the Miami Dolphins eclipsed Joe's record by over 1,000 yards. His passes gained 5,084 yards in 1984.

5: The NFL's St. Louis Cardinals also held his draft rights. The Cardinals offered him $200,000 and a new car, but refused to match the $420,000 contract Joe signed with the Jets.

6: During the early 1970s the White House put Joe's name on an "enemies list." The staffers who compiled the names listed anyone they thought was dangerous to the nation's security. Joe was viewed as a rebel because of his free-and-easy lifestyle. Putting Joe on the list was laughable because he was intensely patriotic. He never spoke out on political or social issues.

7: John Huarte of Notre Dame won the Heisman Trophy in 1964. Huarte, in a strange twist of fate, also signed with the New York Jets in 1965. He received $200,000 for three years, about half of what Joe was paid.

8: With 65 seconds to play, the Jets led, 32-29. At that point NBC cut away from the game in favor of a film called *Heidi*. Fans who wanted to see the end of the game were not enchanted by the switch. Anger turned to outrage when they learned that Oakland had scored two touchdowns in those final, untelevised seconds.

9: Joe does not hold any all-time passing records. Even so, some sportswriters say his 1972 game against the Baltimore Colts was the finest passing performance in football history. Joe threw for 496 yards and six TDs that day against a fine defensive team. When Norm Van Brocklin set the record with 554 yards in 1951, he was playing against a much weaker defense.

10: Each member of the New York Giants took home a winner's check for $36,000. The Buffalo Bills had to content themselves with the loser's share of $18,000 per player.

index